THE SIGNIFICANCE OF
SINCLAIR LEWIS

Photo by Nickolas Muray

Sinclair Lewis

THE SIGNIFICANCE OF SINCLAIR LEWIS

By
STUART P. SHERMAN

 BOOKS FOR LIBRARIES PRESS
FREEPORT, NEW YORK

First Published 1922
Reprinted 1971

INTERNATIONAL STANDARD BOOK NUMBER:
0-8369-5660-5

LIBRARY OF CONGRESS CATALOG CARD NUMBER:
74-148897

PRINTED IN THE UNITED STATES OF AMERICA

THE SIGNIFICANCE of SINCLAIR LEWIS

by STUART P. SHERMAN

As a leader in the famous revolt of the Younger Generation, Mr. Sinclair Lewis is distinguished from many of his coevals by the velocity of his intelligence and the justice of his antipathies. Not quite incidentally, he is conspiring with the spirit of the times to become the most interesting and important novelist in America. Not, as is commonly supposed, a man of one book, he has marked his passage through the stage of brilliant promise by a succession of substantial accomplishments. Yet he is still so young and so brimming with energy, talents, and invention that he impresses one as a man from whom much is to be expected. With all his other gifts, he has that faculty for being opportune which the envious ascribe to luck but which the knowing perceive is a hard-earned acquisition and a part of the open-eyed efficiency of genius. Mr. Lewis is opportune, because he industriously studies himself and his age, like a good humanist, till he understands the needs and aspirations and powers of both. The times in America since the War of the German Invasions have clamored for adequate representation in fiction; with vision of arresting centrality and sharpness, Mr. Lewis is giving it. The publication of his new novel *Babbitt* will set a thousand newspaper reviewers to discussing whether it equals the novel which fluttered their dove-cotes in 1920. It is my purpose rather to indicate the place which *Babbitt* occupies in the succession of Mr. Lewis's books, and to invite somewhat more serious attention to the quality of his work as a whole, and to his significance on the contemporary scene.

When Mark Twain, Henry James, and W. D. Howells died, the wide domain of American realism gaped for a masculine heir. There followed an interval in which no one would read an American who could get a British novel. The field swarmed with claimants who could not be taken seriously, who were just "outside" literature. There was an occasional offering by an old hand, but the "movement" halted for lack of adequate leadership. Poetry was said to be "looking up"—to Mr. Masters and to Miss Lowell, who from different directions had given it fresh impetus. But in prose fiction there seemed to be, say ten years ago, no one "significant" to swear by or to swear at but Mr. Dreiser, a barbarian who has never learned to write English. In their desperation, the critical instigators of our "movement" urged us for a time to look up to Mr. Dreiser. Later they shifted their attention to a more scrupulous artist, Mr. Hergesheimer, who was veering uncertainly between realism and an exotic type of the historical-romantic, and to Mr. Cabell, who had achieved a *succes de scandale* in the erotic-fantastic. From the "lunatic fringe" of experimentation there was an ominous buzzing of "Freudians". Whatever was most unwholesome in the fiction of Russia, France, Germany, and the younger England was cried up by our criticasters and seized upon for imitation. As a fairly direct consequence of the critical encouragement given to bad English and mad psychology, we are now asked to admire such erotic rubbish as Mr. Waldo Frank's *Rahab,* in which a female finds amid the "sickly dissolutions" of the underworld, as Mr. Lewis Mumford tenderly phrases it, "like a rainbow glimmering over a pool of stagnant water, a justification and a light." As I trust even Mr. Menken would say,—"Bosh!" But in the fall of 1920 arrived, to deliver the beleaguered citadel of our hope and sanity, Mr. Sinclair Lewis with *Main Street.*

Now *Main Street,* a criticism of contemporary life with special reference to its interest and beauty, is important to us socially because, more thoroughly than any novel since *Uncle Tom's Cabin,* it has shaken our complacency with regard to the average quality of our civilization. But it and the other work of Mr. Lewis which I shall discuss, are equally important to our literature as a return to the main matter and the manner of our national narrative.

If we had applied ourselves more diligently to the search for a deliverer, we might have observed that Mr. Lewis was coming, far back in 1914, when he published *Our Mr. Wrenn* —as the seductive title suggests, a merrily bubbling story with a "happy ending", somewhat in the vein of H. G. Wells's *Kipps* and *Mr. Polly*. Mr. Wrenn, age thirty-five, sales-entry clerk in the Souvenir and Art Novelty Company of New York, is described as "a meek little bachelor—a person of inconspicuous blue ready-made suits, and a small unsuccessful mustache." What makes this little clerk significant is a rudimentary poetic impulse. With a hunger for adventure stimulated by the moving-pictures, and the work of Mr. Kipling and Jack London, the hero gently revolts from the routine of office, visits England in a cattleboat, and finds romance incarnate in a red-haired art-student in a green crash smock, Istra Nash, who amuses herself with his guileless Philistinism; but he returns in the end to a good domestic Nelly and the evening paper with seven cents' worth of potato salad from the delicatessen shop.

In this, his first picture of Main Street, Mr. Lewis utilizes a formula which is perhaps more or less familiar to students of the *Saturday Evening Post*. But already one can mark his possession of faculties which are to give new interest and seriousness to the ancient tale of the grocer's apprentice. Here is a mastery of the racy American vernacular unequalled since O. Henry flourished; vivid and abundant observation; the realistic "discovery" of the cattle-ship. Here the Middle-Western Rotarian is introduced in a single synoptic sentence:—"an American who had a clipped mustache, brisk manners, a Knight-of-Pythias pin, and a mind for duck-shooting, hardware-selling, and cigars." Here is an imagination which explores with equal success the small mind of Mr. Wrenn superheated in a sales campaign, and the psychology of a frustrated art student from California, cursed with ambition without power. And here finally is a point of view, detached, critical, illumined by the coming spirit—a point of view from which the romantic hunger of Mr. Wrenn and his kind, and the artistic and intellectual aspirations of the girl with red-hair and her kind, can be treated with that "mixture of love and wit," which Thackeray declares is the essence of humor. Says Istra Nash to Mr.

Wrenn, speaking of the Bohemians: "Being Free, of course they're not allowed to go and play with nice people, for when a person is Free, you know, he is never free to be anything but Free". It is a sentence indicative of that early maturing of the critical faculty which distinguishes the first novel of Mr. Lewis from, let us say, the first novel of Mr. Floyd Dell.

His second book, *The Trail of the Hawk*, 1915, is dedicated to "the optimistic rebels, (including his present publisher) through whose talk at luncheon the author watches the many-colored spectacle of life". It is on the surface a story about one of the earlier successful American aviators; but I find, under this curious disguise, the nearest approach that Mr. Lewis has yet made to an "autobiographical" novel, to a revelation of the motives and the influences which have shaped his own career. The imaginative progeny of the realist is of course usually related in some fashion to the seven wrestlers who struggle within himself. The animating passion even of little Mr. Wrenn—his quest for romance in love and travel—Mr. Lewis doubtless found duplicated in his own heart; but in the case of Mr. Wrenn, he diluted the passion and gently caricatured its embodiment. In *The Trail of the Hawk* he treats the same quest but he treats it seriously, and he endows his hero with an important additional passion—the desire for distinction, the love of glory. Carl Ericson of Joralemon, Minnesota, a second-generation Norwegian, is described as "heir-apparent of the age", the typical American of his period: "It was for him to carry on the American destiny of extending the Western horizon; his to restore the wintry Pilgrim virtues and the exuberant, October, partridge-drumming days of Daniel Boone; then to add, in his own or another generation, new American aspirations for beauty."

There is our theme:—the emergence of a typical American from our Middle-Western frontier in the generation who were small boys in 1890. The stages are interesting. First, there is a healthy athletic boyhood in an American small town, where a spark is dropped by a village radical who has read Robert Ingersoll, Karl Marx, and Napoleon—a preliminary sketch of

Bjornstam in *Main Street*. "Life", says this rural philosopher to the boy, "is just a little old checker game played by the alfalfa contingent at the country store unless you've got an ambition that's too big to ever quite lasso it. You want to know that there's something ahead that's bigger and more beautiful than anything you've ever seen". Next comes a course in Plato College, a course terminated abruptly by the boy's open championship of an instructor from Yale who has ruined his usefulness to the institution by discussing the works of H. G. Wells and G. B. Shaw and by admitting the existence of the theory of evolution. There follows a period of miscellaneous adventure as chauffeur, travelling actor, porter on the Bowery, mechanic in the Canal Zone and Mexico, then an apprenticeship in a school of aviation in California, flying for country fairs, a series of prize flights followed by intoxicating ovations, the development of the Touricar company, a love affair on the Palisades and in the Berkshires, respectability and entrance upon contemporary civilization, such as it is, including modern plumbing, individual bed-rooms, candles on the dinner table, Sunday morning breakfasts with choice of conversation or auction-bridge, and the reading of *Tono-Bungay, David Copperfield, Jude the Obscure, The Damnation of Theron Ware, Madame Bovary, McTeague, Walden, War and Peace,* Turgenev, Balzac, and William James. In a free poetic fashion, I assume that this narrative sketches Mr. Lewis's own flight from Sauk Centre, Minnesota, by way of Yale College, New York, and San Francisco journalism, and the short story magazine, into literature.

The Trail of the Hawk is a book with extravagant variety of scenes and atmospheres, the first two-thirds of it written with much gusto. It is important for our study of Mr. Lewis's development as exhibiting the intellectual stuffiness of the stagnating middle-western town, which was the point of departure for his own "revolt". It is still more important as disclosing plainly some of the things which his taste and intelligence recognize as beautiful and desirable. Mr. Lewis is a good hater, but, contrary to the common rumor, he is not all compact of antipathies. He has, I am convinced, a generalized conception of the Good, which, if he were a lyric poet, he could capture in a net of images, like Shelley addressing the Skylark. He likes free air, the swoop of the hawk, arrows that go straight to the mark. Everything that is candid, crisp, fresh, alert, clean, supple, active, and darting, he likes. He has felt the allurement of "beauty with a touch of strangeness"; but he instinctively revolts when beauty is touched with morbidity. From Kipling perhaps he acquired an inclination for purposeful young men who keep themselves fit and are capable of bridging the Ganges, and for young women to match, with temperament controlled by intelligence—of the Beatrice type. Of Istra Nash, who reappears in *The Trail of the Hawk,* he remarks significantly: "She always wants new sensations yet doesn't want to work, and the combination isn't very good." Carl Ericson, the flyer, relishes his adventures, and Mr. Lewis reports them with such sense of flight and clouds and the upper air as I have felt nowhere else save in Mr. Norman Hall's *High Adventure.* But this enterprising young man is notably hard-headed, a hard-worker, with a good workman's prejudice in favor of keeping himself and his tools in order. Mr. Lewis's beauty is always tonic—never relaxing. I remember hearing him say, with a grimace, that he liked best in *Main Street* the purple patches over which he had sweat blood, but that no one else noticed them. His use of landscape is rigorously economical, but there are paragraphs, even in this earlier book, done with a touch that recalls Tolstoy and Turgenev in their great hunting scenes. Here is a whiff of the hero's boyhood in Minnesota:

> He loitered outside the shed, sniffing at the smoke from burning leaves—the scent of autumn and migration and wanderlust. He glanced down between houses to the reedy shore of Joralemon Lake. The surface of the water was smooth, and tinted like a bluebell, save for one patch in the current where wavelets leaped with October madness in sparkles of diamond fire. Across the lake, woods sprinkled with gold-dust and paprika broke the sweep of sparse yellow stubble, and a red barn was softly brilliant in the caressing sunlight and lively air of the Minnesota prairie. Over there was the field of

valor, where grown-up men with shiny shotguns went hunting prairie chickens; the Great World, leading clear to the Red River Valley and Canada.

Three mallard ducks, with necks far out and wings beating hurriedly, shot over Carl's head. From far off a gun-shot floated echoing through forest hollows; in the waiting stillness sounded a rooster's crow, distant, magical.

If Mr. Lewis could "abandon his mind" for a season to landscape and the joy of our American seas and mountains, he could give us our most exhilarating tale of country life. He has the eye and the zest. But as yet he is so jealous of his purely human interest that he is capable of cramming all California into a parenthesis.

There is good writing, there are humor and invention, there are various milieus effectively rendered in Mr. Lewis's first two novels; but in his third, *The Job,* presented in 1917, there are three to four admirable pieces of characterization and a sobriety and firmness of composition which entitle this book to a place next to *Main Street* and *Babbitt.* As he swooped to meet the airmen in 1915, so he swoops, in 1917, to meet the new woman making a career in business. Una Golden of Panama, Pennsylvania, graduate of a business college, who becomes a stenographer in New York, works into suburban real-estate, and then into the assistant-managership of a line of hotels, is, you may say, a typical heroine of the "success" magazines. Agreed:— in a sense, so she is, just as Arnold Bennett's Clayhanger is their hero. The editors of the "success" magazines guiltily share with novelists like Mr. Bennett and Mr. Lewis a sense for recognizing the significant types of our changing civilization. Una Golden differs, however, from the smart short-story writer's girl-with-the-powder-puff as, to take a familiar illustration, Lear's daughters differ from their sketches in Holinshed. She has been seriously and minutely considered. She has been sympathetically and intelligently studied. She has been understood in her pathetic relations to her mother; in her variously irritating relations to a series of employers; in relation to the humdrum suitor that she leaves in Panama, the brilliant young cub who leaves her, the fat-necked voluble commercial traveller whom she marries; in relation, finally, to the intimate inner conflict between her sexual and emotional instincts and her desire to respect herself and to "amount to something". The thing is, as Henry James used to say, "done", and with great precision of stroke. Una Golden lives, and her futile mother. The erratic and "dynamic" young cub, Walter Babson, lives. Eddie Schwirtz, the commercial traveler, a gorgeous beast, lives. And they and dozens of subordinate characters move without confusion through dozens of offices, apartments, boarding-houses, and streets, each eruditely saturated with the appropriate elements of its own atmosphere.

Not an interesting group, till Mr. Lewis became vividly interested in it. What value does he see in Una Golden? What beauty? Well, he sees her as an intelligent and purposeful feminine will emerging from the respectable helplessness and hopelessness of girls who married their first chance and "settled down" in Panama, Pennsylvania—emerging into the beauty of a self-directed life. He sees her as a girl with youth's hunger for enchantment, with arms outstretched for it, missing it, but closing resolutely upon what the wisest among the children of men generally accept as the second best. From the lights of Main Street in Panama, also from certain city lights here flashed upon her, this adventurer derives her "value".

There were a score of mild matter-of-fact Unas on the same Elevated train with her, in their black hats and black jackets and black skirts and white waists, with one hint of coquetry in a white-lace jabot or a white-lace veil; faces slightly sallow or channeled with care, but eyes that longed to flare with love; women whom life didn't want except to type its letters about invoices of rubber heels; women who would have given their salvation for the chance to sacrifice themselves for love . . . And there was one man on that Elevated train, a well-bathed man with cynical eyes, who read a little book with a florid gold cover, all about Clytemnestra, because he was certain that modern cities have no fine romance, no high tragedy; that you must go back to the Greeks for real feeling. He often aphorized, "Frightfully hackneyed to say, 'woman's place is the home,' but really, you know, these women going to offices, vulgarizing all their fine womanliness, and their shrieking sisterhood going in for suffrage and Lord knows what. Give me the reticenses of the harem rather than one of these office-women with gum-chewing vacuities. None of them clever enough to be tragic."

Readers who turn to fiction for "heavenly rest" are not a little disturbed by the presence in all Mr. Lewis's books of certain signs of what is called "social unrest" or, with more overtly hostile intention, "socialistic feeling". Of Una Golden, for example, we are told that, "Into her workaday mind came a low light from the fire which was kindling the world; the dual belief that life is too sacred to be taken in war and filthy industries and dull education; and that most forms and organization and inherited castes are not sacred at all". Now, to the intelligent mind there is really nothing less perturbing than the emergence, in classes and individuals, of intelligence and taste, bespeaking themselves, in an imperfectly adjusted world, to seek their own level. That kind of unrest does not destroy, it creates, the "divine order". The unrest of girls like Una Golden is the hope of the middle-class; and the middle-class, Mr. John Corbin has just assured us, is the hope of our society. From the time of the Rape of the Sabines to the time of Samuel Clemens there has been a danger in unsettled societies that social bandits would dash in from the border and carry off the carefully nurtured daughters of "first families". That danger is the spice of life in a democracy, which offers no more kindling incentive to its undiscovered talents than admission, after due ordeals and the probation of a generation or two, into its first families. I for one regret to observe that our ancient custom of assuring every schoolboy of his right to hope for the Presidency is falling into desuetude—without the slightest visible reason why it should. A novelist who inspires the Younger Generation by reviving this and kindred conceptions of democratic opportunity and reward is restoring one of our invaluable traditions.

I make this solemn transition to *Free Air,* 1919, because it is a "light" novel, constituting a humorous interlude in Mr. Lewis's realistic march. Gravely captious critics may be disposed to dismiss it as a pot-boiler, prepared for the fancy of our touring automobilists. We have frankly admitted that Mr. Lewis is opportune. I do not see how anyone who has ever cranked a Ford can resist this crisp tale of the girl from Brooklyn in her Gomez-Dep roadster and the ingenious young mechanic in his "bug" from Schoenstrom, Minnesota, who discover each other's attraction in an exciting drive by way of Gopher Prairie and the Yellowstone to Seattle, with an engineering education and a Sabine Marriage just ahead. The plot is, indeed, anybody's; but the execution is that of a masterly realist on a lark—not raising any question about the main conventions and conditions of his modern fairy-tale but playing the game with such zest that one almost forgets to enquire whether a nice girl from Brooklyn ever could so far forget herself on a summer vacation as to find anything in common with a garage man. Love as a specialized passion is, as Mr. Lewis treats it in his most serious vein, but a welcome additional zest to companionship in the adventure of life. Here it is but a fillip to the intensely serious consideration of extricating a car from a "morass of prairie gumbo" or piloting it in safety up the last pitch of the continental divide. If in the end Milt Daggett has learned something about the care of his nails from his association with Claire Boltwood, and she something about shifting gears from him; the affair, like the *Beggar's Opera,* is carried off with too light an air to affect subversively the foundations of society.

Main Street, 1920, is another story. Mr. Lewis had been incubating it for six or seven years, though I suspect that his critical faculties were edged for its final revision by his comparative study of American small towns, made on that excursion over the Lincoln Highway, which he so gaily chronicled in *Free Air.* A second novel as deeply rooted in his native soil and in his own past would be as difficult a feat for him as, for their respective authors, a second *Huckleberry Finn,* a second *David Copperfield,* a second *Mill on the Floss,* a second *Pendennis,* a second *Clayhanger.* Like these other five great novels, *Main Street* appears to be the harvest of the writer's best land, which is so often his native heath and the deep impressions of early life, ineffaceable by the lapse of years, and poignantly touching the heart through the revisiting eyes of age. In its exhibition of the interwoven lives of the community, it has the authority, the intimacy, the many-sided insights, the deep saturation of color, which no journalist can ever "get up", which are possible only, one is tempted to say, to one who packs into his book the most vital experience and observation of a lifetime. One must have *lived* that stuff in order to have reproduced it as living organism. And it is with some vague sense that a man can contain only one great autobiography that many readers of *Main Street* have prophesied against Mr. Lewis's future.

To those who wish to believe that they have found not merely a new novel but also a new novelist, capable of fresh flights for distance and altitude, certain reassuring considerations may be presented. *Main Street,* unlike three-fourths of the novels of the day, is not autobiographical. It is to an extraordinary degree an objective representation of contemporary society extended through a period of not more than half-a-dozen years. In this society Mr. Lewis himself has not a single "personal representative." Neither Dr. Kennicot, nor Carol, nor Guy Pollock, nor Vida Sherwin, nor Sam Clark, nor Percy Breshnahan, nor Erik Valborg, nor Miles Bjornstam, nor Fern Mullins, nor Mrs. Bogart is his "register". Each one of these persons is a perfectly distinct individual with firm centre and contours honestly constructed after innumerable observations and hard, earnest work of the realistic imagination. Mr. Lewis will not exhaust his material while he retains his present capacity for research. Deeply indebted as he may be to Mr. Wells for the illumination of his point of view as an observer of the human spectacle, he has studied the art of constructing the novel under other masters with far greater respect for their profession than that famous producer who semi-annually charges a new lay figure with the task of communicating to the world the latest state of his own consciousness. The contemporary English novelist whose best work is most nearly comparable with *Main Street* is Mr. Bennett in *The Old Wives' Tale* and *Clayhanger*. But the book from which, I should say, Mr. Lewis without losing a particle of his own idiom or the independence of his American vision, has learned his most valuable "secrets" is *Madame Bovary*.

Both *Main Street* and *Madame Bovary* are mordantly critical representations of contemporary civilization. In each case, the criticism is intensely focussed upon the bourgeois society of a representative provincial town. In each case, the "hero" is a country doctor, who is, thanks to an insensitive aesthetic organization, sufficiently content with his lot and in love with his young wife. In each case, the "heroine" has been touched by literature and contact with the city to revolt against the Philistinism of her husband and the restrictions of her life, in behalf of romantic ideals of which she is unable to find any worthy incarnations. In each case, the searching criticism which plays over the scene and the actors is delivered indirectly by an intricate system of contrasts and the cross-lighting and reflected lighting of subordinate characters. I will add an observation which many readers fail to make: Flaubert was in love with Emma and Mr. Lewis is in love with Carol; and both authors analyze and expose the object of their affection with a merciless rigor which no woman can either understand or pardon—she can understand the rigor but not the love which inflicts it and survives it. They treat their heroes with similar austerity—with the difference that Flaubert despises his, and the American author does not. To the student of Mr. Lewis's indirect analytical method, I commend his remorseless twenty-fourth chapter, beginning with the "thesis": "All that midsummer month Carol was sensitive to Kennicot"; likewise his subtle record of Carol's reaction to Breshnahan in relation to her husband. So much for the parallelism between the French master and the American disciple.

As for the divergence, it is not all to the advantage of Flaubert. Mr. Lewis saw more types of people, more kinds of activity, more meshes of the social network in Gopher Prairie than Flaubert saw in Rouen. Without destroying their artistic subordination, he made more of his secondary personages. He increased greatly the significance and the tension of his novel by choosing, as the principal representatives of middle-class revolt and middle-class stability, characters with a far higher degree of general and professional intelligence than is possessed by the French protagonists. He faithfully presents the specific erotic passion as only occasionally or seasonally perturbing the average American temperament—not obsessing it, not hounding it. Flaubert sees this passion as the centre of his theme. Mr. Lewis does not. If our novelists generally were not dissuaded by the terrors of our censorship, if they dared to tell the truth, would they like many of their European colleagues and like one or two of their American confreres, would they represent the average middle-class American as living feverishly from one liaison to the next? Mr. Lewis does not appear to think so. Dr. Kennicot had, before his marriage, been around "with the boys" and perhaps he never became utterly incapable of a slip; but I doubt whether Mr. Lewis has been guilty of any important suppression of the truth in declaring that his mind was absorbed in his five hobbies: medicine, land-investment, Carol, motoring, and hunting. (As for Carol—that well-turned, dynamic, rather intensely feminine, too taut a young woman whom I meet with greater frequency each year, flinging her coat into chairs and "exploding" into other living rooms than those of Gopher Prairie, to the disgust of the stodgy and to the delight and the refreshment of the others—; she might be more simply happy or more simply miserable if the sex instincts were stronger in her; if she could content herself with being either mother, wife or mistress; if she could repeat *ex animo* that sweet and wistfully cadenced Mid-Victorian line which, alas, I have forgotten, to the effect that love is only an incident in a man's life—" 'tis a woman's whole existence"—something like that.)

When I found that I had forgotten the exact words of this phrase, which in my youth I have heard a hundred times on plaintive lips, I went to some friends one generation older than mine, and confidently asked them to recall it. I wanted it, as you see, to conclude the preceding paragraph. But they too, had forgotten it, or they remember it, rather, as I remember it—as something that people used to repeat, or as something that Robert Browning might have excogitated in meditating on the early life of that eminent early Victorian, the authoress of *Aurora Leigh*. The oblivion which is overtaking this "familiar quotation" is a straw indicating a shifting of the winds of social change. The words no longer give an echo to the seat where modern love is throned. Opportunities for women opened by the war, the steady stimulation of middle-class daughters by the state universities, and various other causes are making the situation of intelligent girls marooned in our innumerable Gopher Prairies appear to them acutely painful and almost intolerable. The clear-eyed and hard-headed ones see in time, and the others too late for easy solution of their problems, that a girl who lets love become her "whole existence" is snared, excluded from the special interests and activities of her age, and in a fair way to become tedious to her husband and to herself. In this new middle-class society which is forming around them, the clear-eyed and hard-headed ones perceive that abstract "womanhood" is destined to receive less lip-service and specific women more attention than they have received in the past. The woman who counts, like the man who counts, will be esteemed more and more for the developed virtues of her own individuality, whatever they may be, and less and less frequently conceived of as a "skirt", whatever its quality. Now so far as *Main Street* is "the story of Carol Kennicot", it shows an eager young creature beating her luminous wings rather wildly, as young creatures do, yet not without some sense of the direction in which light and freedom are. A "back-yard" affair with Erik Valborg—that for example, she discovers decisively, is not the way out. That might be an alleviant to the yearnings of Emma Bovary but it would not be even a temporary sop to her. With true insight into the significant aspect of the present unrest among young women, the revolt of Carol is shown to have very little relation with the much-advertised movement for "sexual freedom". Carol is, on the contrary, rebellious precisely at the fetters which accepting such things of sex as a "woman's whole existence" has imposed upon her. Her revolt is inspired by a general hunger of the heart for its own development through appropriate activities of hand and will and brain. In so far as this is true, I judge her revolt to be not only significant but beautiful and not altogether hopeless, as I should attempt to show if I had space to discuss the "improvable greatness" of Mr. Kennicot and to prognosticate his wife's ultimate discovery of it and their transmission of their complementary virtues to their offspring.

But that, adequately done, would demand another novel, dealing with the Kennicots of the second generation, which I hope Mr. Lewis will write when that generation has revealed itself to him.

At present, however, while his satirical powers at their height, the young people who are just emerging from college may be congratulated that his devastating searchlight is still playing upon the middle-aged. His new novel *Babbitt* is not a sequel to *Main Street* but a parallel and coordinate extension. It is a picture of contemporary American society not in the small towns and villages but in the cities of some numerical pretentions. Zenith, the prosperous middle-western city of 350,000, in which George F. Babbitt, the prosperous "realtor" establishes himself on Floral Heights, is inhabited largely by people who had in their youth ambition enough to get up and get out of the "hick burgs". They flatter themselves that, leaving behind them all the elements that constituted the dinginess and dreariness of Gopher Prairie, they have pressed forward to the mark of the high calling of hustling, right-thinking, forward-looking boosters, good-fellows, and 100% Americans. For Iron they have substituted copper sinks in the kitchen; for the Saturday night tubbing, the daily bath; for golden-oak, near-mahogany; for the Ford the limousine; for the dirty, ramshackle, huddle of shops and visibly suspendered tobacco-chewing shopkeepers blocks of aspiring office buildings and hotels with manicure girls attending in the Pompeian Barber Shop; for the somnolent barn-like church an up-to-date competitive "community centre" with press-agents, military organization, and pep-masters; for cigars and poker in the parlor with Sam Clark and "the boys" monogrammed cigarettes and mixed auction bridge at the country club; for "open meetings" of the Thanatopsis society week-end parties with prohibition anecdotes and cocktails.

With comprehensive and mordant notation of detail coupled with a formidable power of generalization, Mr. Lewis shows how the city attempts to solve the problem of the small town. Between Gopher Prairie and Zenith, there is the material progress of a generation—a long march in America. But between Gopher Prairie and Zenith, civilization, according to this record,—civilization, judged by the decisive tests—has not advanced an inch. The quantity of human happiness has not increased, nor has its quality improved. The people are not more open-minded, nor more upright, nor more beautiful, nor more interesting. This is not "the story of Carol", and the unrest among young women, which she so vividly illustrated, finds here no adequate representative. The "leading lady" does not lead. Myra Babbitt, Mrs. George F., is a woman, "definitely mature", who has, in a dull fashion, accepted her universe: "She was a good woman, a kind woman, a diligent woman, but no one, save perhaps Tinka her ten-year old, was at all interested in her or entirely aware that she was alive"—a tragical sentence, applicable enough to the average middle-class American woman of forty. But this is primarily a story of a man's unrest. This is the story of Babbitt; the graduate of a state university, the "swaddled American husband", the prosperous American broker, the Rotarian, the leading citizen, the consequence and cause of civilization as it exists in Zenith, and the embodiment of nearly all its vices and its virtues.

Babbitt is a more important character than Dr. Kennicot in that he is more nearly ubiquitous. Less trustworthy as a man, he will perhaps be found more interesting as a "hero" because he has less of character and more of temperament. Unlike the Doctor, he is highly self-conscious, he has a "soft" streak, he is an egotist, and he is eager for the applause and admiration of men and women, not excluding his wife, for whom he feels an habitual tolerance, and including his stenographer, whom he wishes to impress as a "great man", and his manicurist, to whom he is willing, in relaxed and erratic moods, to appear as a person with possibilities of romance. In the morning Mr. Babbitt wears a well-made, well-pressed grey suit with white piping on the V of the vest. In the evening he wears, when there is important company, a "Tuxedo" which Mrs. Babbitt vainly insists that he should call a "dinner-jacket"—that is the precise "note" of their social status. He is diligent in business and not more crooked than William Washington Eathorne, President of the First State Bank, a chilly old gentleman who lives in an old brick house of the Civil War period, and who impresses Babbitt as "the real thing" by quietly ringing for a whiskey toddy, instead of mooing and baying around the subject, as in his own circle is the custom when the host produces something illicit from the ice-box.

This is one of the many incidents by which Mr. Lewis illustrates the peculiar pathos of his hero's situation. With all that the civilization of Zenith can offer at his disposal, Babbitt is restless and unsatisfied. He has money enough, things enough, physical comforts enough. He has, like great numbers of our prosperous middle-class, reached the point where the multiplication of things gives no addition of content. There is a gnawing hunger in him but he can think of nothing that he wants to eat. In a vague way he desires "the right thing" for himself, for his family, for his community; but there is no authoritative standard, there is no one to tell him, there is nothing in the society of Zenith to show him by example, what the "real right thing" is. Consequently, in the restlessness of satiety and inner boredom, Babbitt 'unintelligently and unimaginatively gropes for his missing felicity in unfruitful directions: in imitating Mr. Eathorne, in speechmaking and prominence at business men's conventions, in running off to the Maine woods where one can wear old clothes and chew tobacco and "cuss" in freedom, and finally in various experiments in marital infidelity. But from all these ventures he returns with the taste of sand and ashes in his mouth. And the only gleam that lights the final pages of the book is his indulgent humor towards his children, one of whom is studying the drama and labor statistics, while the other, his son, has just revealed his secret off-hand marriage. To the boy he says:

> "Practically I've never done a single thing I've wanted to in my whole life. I don't know's I've accomplished anything except just get along. . . . Well, maybe you'll carry things on further. I don't know. But I do get a kind of sneaking pleasure out of the fact that you knew what you wanted to do and did it. Well, those folks in there will try to bully you, and tame you down. Tell 'em to go to the devil! I'll back you. Take your factory job, if you want to. Don't be scared of the family. No, nor all of Zenith. Nor of yourself, the way I've been. Go ahead, old man! The world is yours!"

I have no high expectation regarding Babbitt's son. He gives as little promise as his father of capacity for finding delight in the things of the mind. The daughter may conceivably become an interesting individual, perhaps only an intense and difficult one.

Babbitt is not a representation of the highest American standards of morals and manners. But neither is *The Rise of Silas Lapham* nor *Huckleberry Finn* nor Henry James's *The American*. Neither is *Vanity Fair* a representation of the highest standards of morals and manners in England, nor is *David Copperfield,* nor *Pride and Prejudice.* It is not the business of the realistic novelist nor dramatist, to confine his studies to those small and isolated spots in which the society of his contemporaries approaches perfection. To propose such an aim is absurd. A jury of award which accepted it would at once be obliged to exclude from its consideration practically everything that is worth considering. In the age of Elizabeth the acceptance of such an aim would have excluded from consideration the chief tragedies of Shakespeare and all the comedies of **Ben Jonson.** The most important business of the capable painter of contemporary society from Balzac to the present day has been the portrayal of the great representative types. In an immense and motley democracy booming furiously through the stages of material progress, few of the great representative types know anything about the "highest standard of manners and morals in America".

All that we may fairly demand of our novelists—and it is a large demand—is that they themselves, as observers of the human spectacle, should be aware of this "highest standard", should paint their great representative types at a point of view at which the best society is at least within their vision. It is a large demand but it is a fair demand to make of a class of men who undertake to govern us through our imaginations. It is a fair demand to make of men whose profession involves a connoisseurship of truth and beauty. It is a necessary demand, if their criticism of life is to have any social value. *Vanity Fair,* for example, though it is for the most part a picture of a selfish and disagreeable world, is obviously written by a man who understands what an unselfish and agreeable world might be, while Mr. Dreiser's *Genius,* for another example, is a picture of a selfish and disagreeable world, written by a man incapable of conceiving anything else.

Now Mr. Lewis, with increasing clearness of apprehension and vitality of presentment has devoted himself to the portrayal of the representative. There is no denying the vigor or the representativeness of the types presented in *The Job, Main Street,* and *Babbitt.* Nor is there doubt in anyone's mind that Mr. Lewis's contemporary scene is drenched in irony and raked with satire. The one rather serious objection which one hears raised against his work is that the standards, the existence of which are implied in any consistently satiric picture of society,—the standards by which Mr. Lewis judges, for instance, Gopher Prairie and Zenith are not sufficiently in evidence. The publication of *Babbitt* is likely to increase the frequency of that objection; for while in *Main Street,* there are at least four persons, including Carol, with quite definite conceptions of what ought to be done to increase beauty and interest in Gopher Prairie, in *Babbitt* these quite definite improvements have been made, without essential increase of beauty or interest in the lives of the citizens; and no one in the book seems to understand what to do next. We are on the brink of a Tolstoian problem. The artistic charm and vivacity of this novel, to say nothing of its social stimulation, would have been heightened by somewhat freer employment of those devices of dramatic contrast of which Mr. Lewis is a master—by the introduction of some character or group capable of reflecting upon the Babbitts oblique rays from a social and personal felicity, more genuine, more inward than any of the summoned witnesses possesses. Eventually, if Mr. Lewis does not wish to pass for a hardened pessimist, he will have to produce a hero qualified to register in some fashion the results of his own quest for the desirable; he will have to give us his Portrait of a Lady, his Pendennis, his Warrington and his Colonel Newcome. Meanwhile I am very well content to applaud the valor of his progress through Vanity Fair.

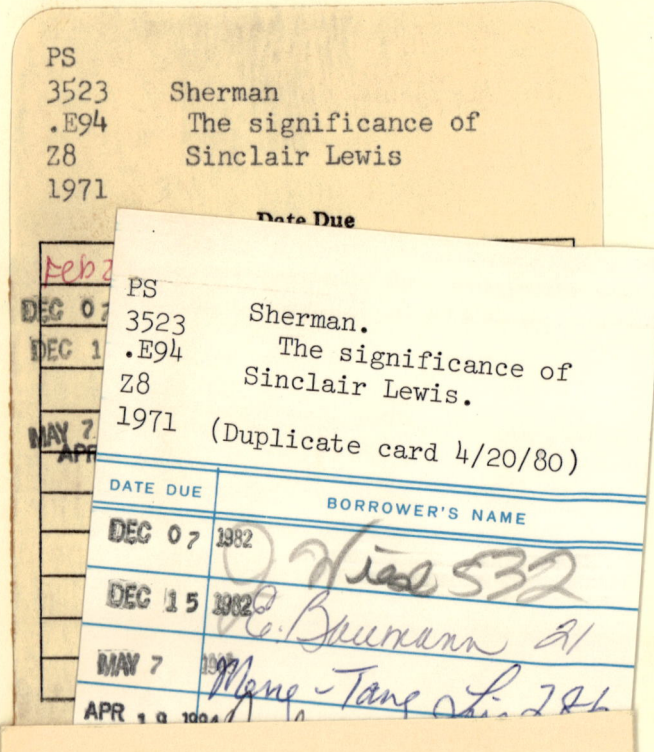